Maria Koran

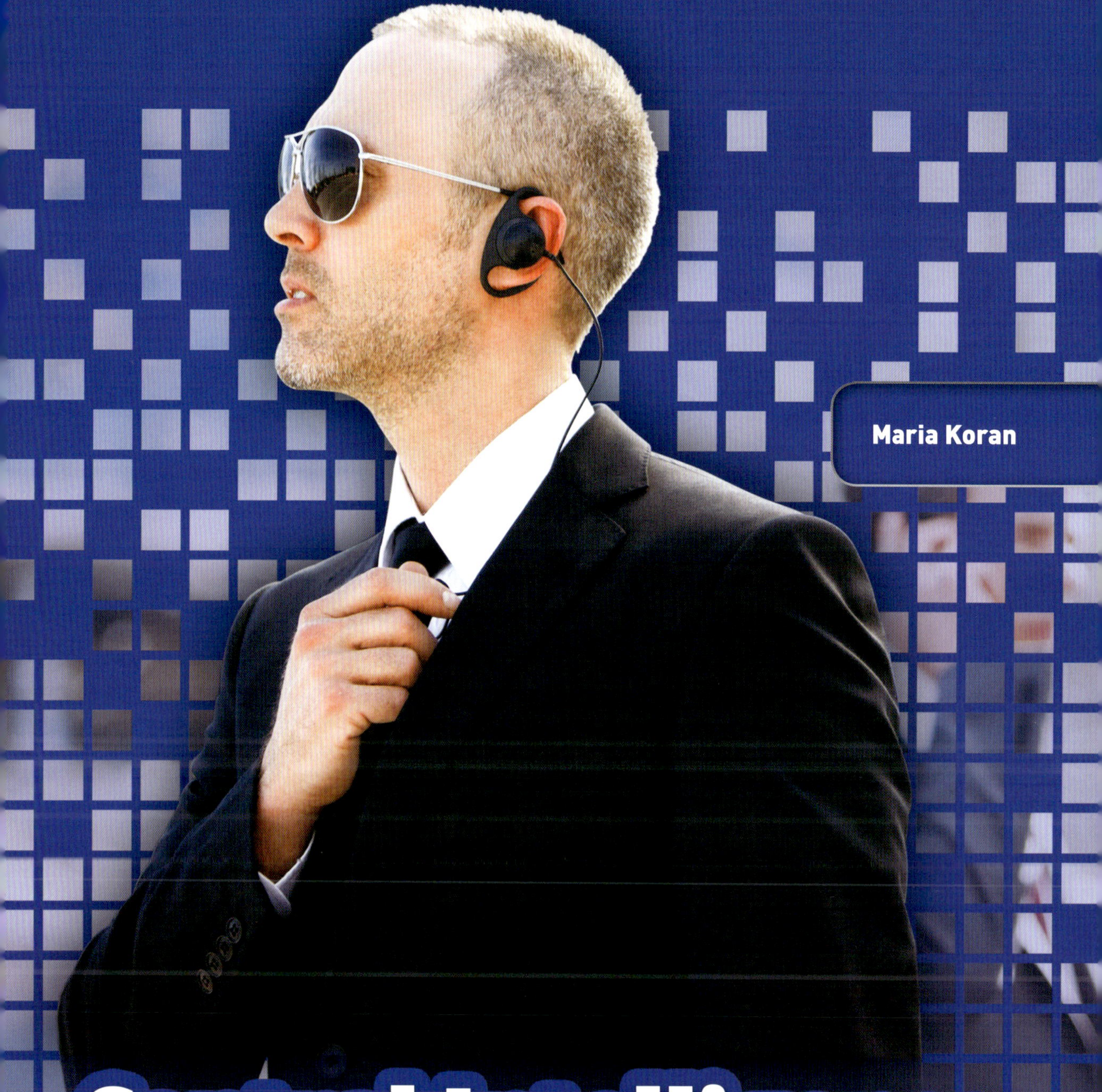

Central Intelligence Agency

POWER • AUTHORITY • GOVERNANCE

LIGHTBOX
openlightbox.com

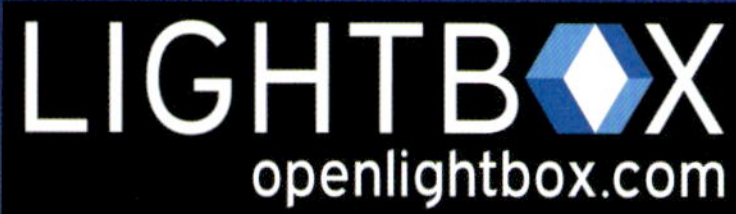

Go to
www.openlightbox.com
and enter this book's
unique code.

ACCESS CODE

LBXV7557

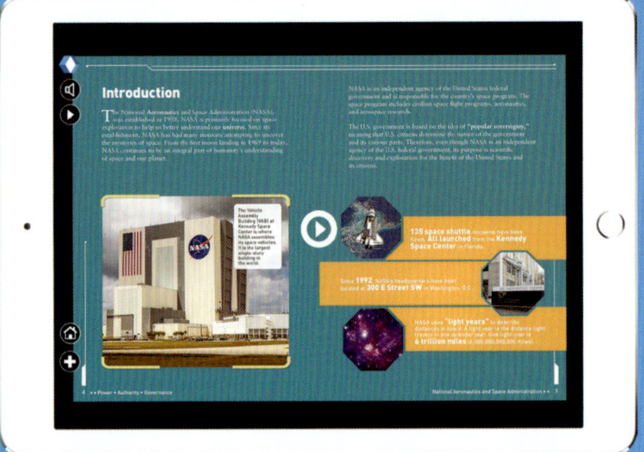

Lightbox is an all-inclusive digital solution for the teaching and learning of curriculum topics in an original, groundbreaking way. Lightbox is based on National Curriculum Standards.

STANDARD FEATURES OF LIGHTBOX

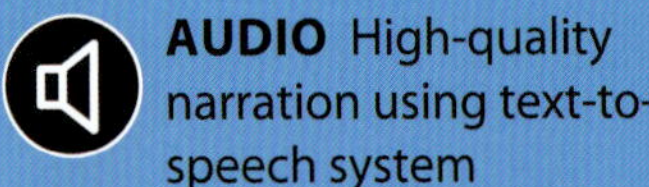
AUDIO High-quality narration using text-to-speech system

VIDEOS Embedded high-definition video clips

ACTIVITIES Printable PDFs that can be emailed and graded

WEBLINKS Curated links to external, child-safe resources

SLIDESHOWS Pictorial overviews of key concepts

TRANSPARENCIES Step-by-step layering of maps, diagrams, charts, and timelines

INTERACTIVE MAPS Interactive maps and aerial satellite imagery

QUIZZES Ten multiple choice questions that are automatically graded and emailed for teacher assessment

KEY WORDS Matching key concepts to their definitions

MORE Extra information and details on the subject

FIRST HAND Letters, diaries, and other primary sources

DOCS Speeches, newspaper articles, and other historical documents

Copyright © 2020 Smartbook Media Inc. All rights reserved.

POWER • AUTHORITY • GOVERNANCE

Central Intelligence Agency

CONTENTS

Introduction

The Central Intelligence Agency (CIA) is the U.S. agency that is responsible for gathering information about foreign nations. However, it does much more. The CIA studies that information to understand what it means. Then, it explains it to our national leaders so they can make good decisions. Some of this information is **classified.**

It is the CIA's job to help keep the U.S. safe. One of the ways they do that is by stopping foreign agents from learning our national secrets. This is called **counterintelligence**. The CIA does not make policy. That is up to our elected leaders.

The CIA is not a law enforcement agency. It cannot arrest people. It is the CIA's job to protect the United States from any threat that might want to hurt us. That could be a hostile nation, or it could be a **terrorist**. The CIA has to know what other countries may want to do to hurt the United States and stop them.

Construction on the CIA's Original Headquarters Building (OHB) began in 1959. The building's cornerstone contains a time capsule.

The U.S. government is based on the idea of **"popular sovereignty."** The U.S. citizens give power and authority to the government. All parts of the government serve the will of the people. The CIA has great authority and power. However, even it must obey certain rules. These rules and laws come from the U.S. Constitution.

The CIA must be careful when investigating threats to the United States. It is against the law for the CIA to investigate a U.S. citizen on U.S. soil. The CIA must respect a citizen's right to privacy. This right is guaranteed by the Fourth Amendment to the Constitution.

The CIA was born from the **Office of Strategic Services (OSS)**. The OSS was ahead of its time in equal rights and was **35 percent** women.

The CIA's current headquarters building is in Langley, Virginia. On **April 26, 1999**, the complex was renamed the **George Bush Center for Intelligence.**

Spying has been a part of U.S. history since the country began. In **1780**, Benedict Arnold was identified as a spy for the British during the **Revolutionary War**.

Origins of the CIA

By 1942, the United States had been attacked by Japan, and Germany had declared war on us. We were fighting in World War II. The nation needed information about our enemies. The Office of Strategic Services (OSS) was formed on June 13, 1942. People, both men and women, were needed to gather information about the enemy. These new agents were sent to North Africa, Europe, China, Burma, and India - anywhere they could learn about the enemy.

President Truman signed a document called the National Security Act to create the CIA.

However, not everyone was happy with this new secret agency. The Department of State and the armed services insisted that President Roosevelt keep many of the war's most important secrets away from the OSS. Even the FBI prevented the OSS from working on U.S. soil. This made the OSS invent their own ways of gathering and studying information. Over time, the OSS grew to more than 13,000 people. Those brave men and women fought hard to help us win the war.

Still, no one thought that the OSS would continue after the war. On September 20, 1945 President Harry Truman ordered the OSS to shut down. Its leader, General William Donovan, was asked to stay and help with the change. The OSS became a much smaller Strategic Services Unit (SSU). After the SSU was created, General Donovan was asked to leave. The OSS was finished.

However, the need for intelligence grew. In January 1946, a new office was created, the Central Intelligence Group (CIG). However, it was still under command of the State Department and the armed services. To free itself from outside control, the CIG convinced President Truman to make it the independent Central Intelligence Agency on September 18, 1947.

Branches of Government

The CIA is an independent agency. However, it also must report to other authorities. The director of the CIA reports to the Director of National Intelligence (DNI). The DNI reports to the president.

The U.S. government is organized so that no branch has unlimited authority. This is known as "checks and balances." Although the CIA has a great deal of power, it is "checked" by both the **legislative** branch and the judicial branch.

Congress has the authority to request information from the CIA about its operations. Congress controls the CIA's budget. That is a powerful check. If the CIA refuses, Congress can remove funding from the agency.

Purpose of the CIA

The purpose of the CIA is to keep U.S. citizens safe. It protects us from foreign attacks. It provides the president with information about foreign countries and their leaders. To do this, the CIA gathers intelligence from all over the world, from many sources, and studies it.

The CIA provides information to national leaders including the president's cabinet.

The CIA cannot investigate U.S. citizens on U.S. soil. It can only work inside the United States if it works with another agency such as the FBI or the Department of Homeland Security (DHS). It must obey all U.S. rules and laws. Its agents are sworn to be honest and truthful in their work.

The CIA provides the president and other decision makers with correct, clear information. It learns as much as possible about what is going on in foreign countries. This is often very dangerous work. The CIA also works with friendly countries to help them. By helping friendly countries, the CIA hopes to keep the world safer. This is good for everyone. Unfortunately, we often need information on our enemies more than our friends.

CIA agents often work overseas.

An important part of a CIA agent's job is to protect sources that give them information. This means that agents must keep secrets. One of the secrets agents must keep is the fact that they even work for the CIA.

The Fourth Amendment

The Fourth Amendment to the U.S. Constitution was introduced by James Madison in 1789. This amendment was part of the Bill of Rights that was added to the Constitution.

The Fourth Amendment was designed to protect U.S. citizens from unreasonable searches and seizures of their property. This protection is often called the "Right to Privacy."

The job of the CIA is to gather information from foreign sources that might affect the safety of U.S. citizens. Sometimes this information leads back to people living in the United States. This leads to an important discussion of the role of the CIA versus the rights of U.S. citizens. If the CIA receives information that indicates that a U.S. citizen might be doing something that could harm other people, should the CIA be able to spy on them?

The protections of the Fourth Amendment are something that the CIA take very seriously as they do their job of protecting U.S. citizens.

CIA Through the Years

The CIA was created more than 50 years ago. Since then, it has been involved in many major events in U.S. history. Although the agency has changed through the years, it remains an important part of the U.S. government.

December 7, 1941

The United States enters World War II after the Japanese bomb the American fleet in Pearl Harbor, Hawai'i.

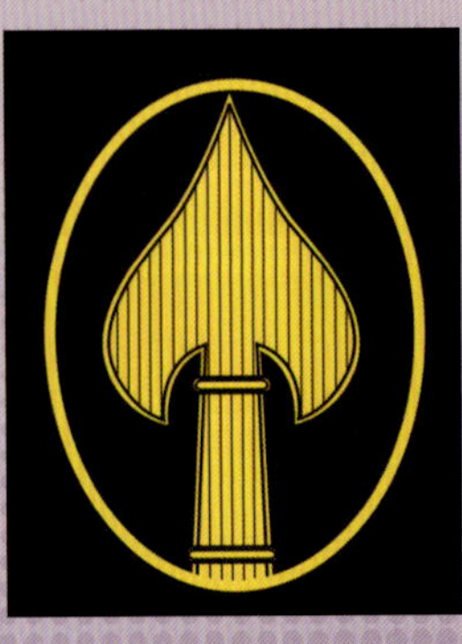

June 13, 1942

The Office of Strategic Services (OSS) is founded.

September 18, 1947

The CIA is founded.

1947

The United States enters a **"Cold War"** with the **Soviet Union** from 1947 to 1991.

1956

The first U2 spy plane flies over the Soviet Union.

1961

The CIA and U.S. Air Force form an office to manage **reconnaissance** satellites.

September 17, 1978

The Camp David Accords are signed, bringing peace between Egypt and Israel. Information from the CIA helps during negotiations.

December 21, 1988

Libyan terrorists blow up Pan Am flight 103 over Lockerbie, Scotland. The CIA and FBI join with European agencies to investigate.

November 9, 1989

The Berlin Wall is destroyed. This begins the end of the Cold War between the United States and the Soviet Union.

August 2, 1990

Operation Desert Storm begins after Iraq invades Kuwait.

2008

The position of Director of National Intelligence is created.

2010

Ten Russian **spies** are arrested in the United States. All plead guilty.

2011

Osama bin Laden is killed. The CIA worked with many other organizations around the world to help locate him.

2017

The CIA releases 470,000 documents recovered from the raid on Osama bin Laden.

CIA Issues

CIA agents risk their lives to protect the United States. The majority of agents do their jobs honestly and truthfully. However, there have been times when a few agents have gone too far or have broken the law.

Sometimes, a CIA agent has killed a citizen of a foreign country in that person's home country. Murder is illegal in every country. When people find out that such an action was committed by a U.S. agent, it causes serious trouble. Relations with that country can become very difficult. The CIA cannot do its job without cooperation from other countries.

In a few instances, CIA agents have broken U.S. laws. They spied on citizens inside the United States. However, the CIA is not allowed to spy on citizens on U.S. soil. In addition, some of these spying situations were because of the citizen's race. This was a serious violation of civil rights. The agents involved were punished. However, it made cooperation between the CIA and other agencies more difficult because the CIA agents had broken trust.

The Patriot Act, passed in 2001, greatly expanded the scope of surveillance allowed under U.S. law.

Finally, some CIA agents have spied against the United States for enemy countries. Those cases caused enormous damage to our intelligence agencies and threatened national safety. These **"double-agents"** were caught and put in jail, but not before the damage was done.

The CIA has learned from many of its mistakes. It now has much stricter rules on what CIA agents can do. These rules apply in both foreign countries and here in the United States.

Checks and Balances

The CIA was involved in many secret operations throughout the Cold War with the Soviet Union. Because of this secrecy, the U.S. government realized that it was important to have very clear rules on what the CIA can do in another foreign country.

There were two main points that the U.S. government wanted to make very clear. The first was that the CIA did not have the authority to spy on U.S. citizens within the borders of the United States. The second point was that the CIA did not have the authority to kill members of any foreign government.

On December 4, 1981, President Ronald Reagan signed Executive Order 12333. This executive order specifically addressed these two main points. It also gave clear guidance on how the other departments of government should cooperate with the CIA to help it do its job.

An executive order is a directive from the president that becomes law. The president is granted this authority by Article Two of the Constitution.

Key Figures in the CIA

An agency as important as the CIA must have had many important people as its director. While agents must keep their identities a secret, the director is the public face of the agency.

Roscoe H. Hillenkoetter

Admiral Roscoe H. Hillenkoetter (1897–1982) was the third director of the Central Intelligence Group (CIG), and the third director of the Department of Central Intelligence (DCI). He was also the first director of the new Central Intelligence Agency (CIA).

Allen Dulles

Allen Dulles (1893–1969) became the first civilian to head the CIA in 1952. Non-military, Dulles was both an attorney and a U.S. **diplomat**. He was the agency's director longer than anyone. Dulles Airport in Washington, D.C. was named after him.

Gina Haspel

Gina Haspel (1956–) is the current director of the CIA. She is also the first woman to hold the position. She joined the agency in 1985. Haspel worked in many countries and became the Station Chief in several secret locations before becoming director.

Bay of Pigs Invasion

HISTORICAL CASE STUDY

In 1959, Fidel Castro's forces won a civil war in the country of Cuba. Shortly after coming to power, Castro asked the Soviet Union for support and aid. Castro turned Cuba into a communist country.

The CIA created a plan to overthrow Castro. They would train 1,400 Cubans who had fled Castro to fight and win back their country. The United States would also militarily support them after the Cubans had invaded.

However, the plan was known in Cuban communities in Florida. Cuban spies told Castro about the plot to remove him. The Cuban army was ready for the coming battle.

The plan was for the Cubans to invade their home country at the "Bay of Pigs." However, CIA airstrikes to soften up Cuban defenses failed. When the invaders landed on the beach, the Cuban Air Force and Army were waiting for them. Most of the invaders were killed and the rest were taken prisoner. The Bay of Pigs ruined the hopes for peace between the United States and Cuba.

Fidel Castro was the leader of Cuba from 1959 to 2008.

Careers in the CIA

Operations Officer

These are the CIA workers that are often known as "spies." Operations officers spend most of their time overseas. They get to know people and learn about that country. They often work alone. The intelligence they gather is the heart and soul of CIA work. An operations officer can be posted anywhere in the world.

Language Officer

CIA language officers use their foreign language skills and knowledge of cultures. They translate languages for the CIA. A language officer is usually stationed in Washington, D.C., but they can travel overseas. The CIA depends on them for important information.

Graphic Designer

Graphic designers make visual aids. Those aids help people such as law makers, the military, and even the president of the United States understand information. CIA graphic designers know some of the most important secrets. They need to figure out how to present them visually.

Data Scientist

Data scientists are the backbone of the CIA. They organize intelligence, study it, and make sense of it. A data scientist's results are shown to U.S. decision makers. They must be up-to-date with the latest technology. They must be able to see patterns in the data that most people cannot.

The CIA's budget is a government secret and **classified**. No U.S. civilian knows what it is.

If the director of the CIA must leave his post, the **deputy director** takes over the position until a new director is confirmed.

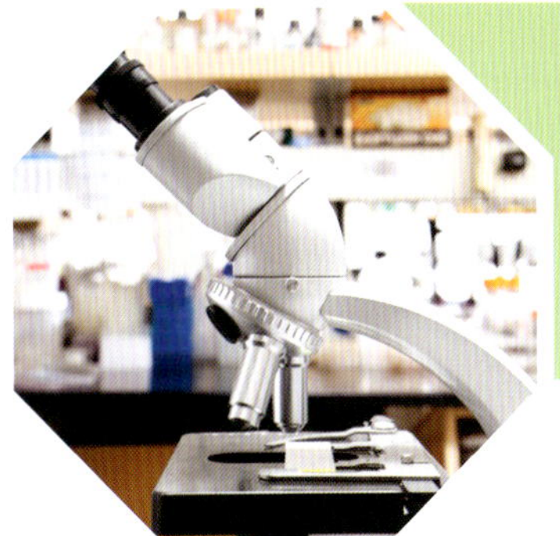

STEM stands for Science, Technology, Engineering, and Math. The CIA has **35** STEM related careers.

Tools of the Trade

The CIA needs many different tools and devices to do its job. Unlike spies from the movies, most CIA agents never carry a gun. Most of these tools are better for the job.

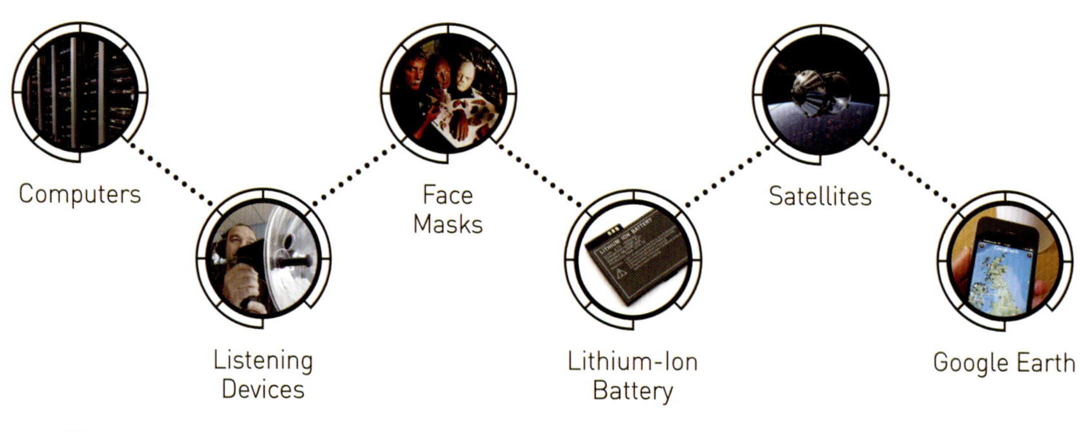

Computers

The CIA gathers most of its information from computers, not spies. Computers are also used to help analyze the information. In fact, the CIA has developed some of the most advanced computers and programs in the world. However, many of these tools are kept secret.

Listening Devices

Enemies of the United States want to keep their plans secret. The CIA has developed very sensitive listening devices that can hear conversations through thick glass and walls. In this way, the targets never know they were overheard. This is an important way to get information.

Face Masks

Sometimes an agent needs to hide their identity. The CIA has people who make life-like masks of the human face. These masks are rarely used, but they are useful tools for the CIA when needed.

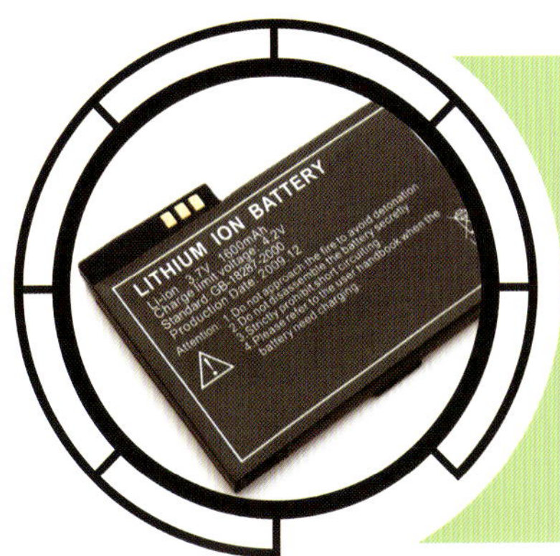

Lithium-Ion Battery

The CIA needed a battery that was powerful, lasted a long time, and was very small. They were successful, but it was so technologically advanced they kept it a secret for years. Today the lithium-ion battery invented by the CIA powers everything from smart phones to medical equipment.

Satellites

Satellites orbit the Earth hundreds of miles overhead. However, their cameras can read a license plate from outer space. By using satellites, the CIA can avoid sending an agent into a dangerous or unknown area to gather important information.

Google Earth

The CIA and other agencies worked with the private Keyhole company to develop the Google Earth project. This software allows you to see anywhere in the world. It is now even used in elementary schools.

CIA in North America

The CIA has offices across the United States. They work with other agencies including the FBI and DHS to help protect against international terrorism.

1

San Francisco, California

In 2017, the threat of a terrorist attack forced half of the Golden Gate Bridge to close during the San Francisco Marathon. The CIA and other agencies advised the race officials about terrorist threats. It was the first time the bridge had ever been closed for the race.

2

New York, New York

On February 26, 1993 a truck heavily loaded with explosives blew up in the underground parking garage of the World Trade Center. The CIA worked with other agencies to find the men involved.

CANA
UNITED STATE
MEX
Washington
Montana
Oregon
Idaho
Wyoming
Nevada
Utah
Colorado
California
Arizona
New Mexico
Pacific Ocean

LEGEND

- Land (USA)
- Land (Other)
- Water

SCALE

400 MILES

700 KILOMETERS

3
Langley, Virginia
The CIA headquarters is located in Langley. It replaced the Original Headquarters Building, which is simply referred to as "OHB." The OHB is now a museum and is open for tours.
New Hampshire
Vermont
Maine
Massachusetts
Rhode Island
Connecticut
New Jersey
Delaware
Maryland
District of Columbia
North Dakota
South Dakota
Minnesota
Wisconsin
Michigan
New York
2
Pennsylvania
Ohio
Indiana
Illinois
Iowa
Nebraska
Kansas
Missouri
West Virginia
3
Virginia
Kentucky
North Carolina
Tennessee
South Carolina
Oklahoma
Arkansas
Alabama
Georgia
Mississippi
Texas
Louisiana
Florida
Atlantic Ocean
N
W
E
S
Gulf of Mexico
LAUNCH POSITION
MISSILE-READY TENTS
MISSILE ERECTORS
4
4
Cuba
In 1962, U.S. aircraft took photos over Cuba. They showed nuclear missiles on the island. The CIA helped study the information and advised President Kennedy about the situation. It came to be known as the Cuban Missile Crisis.

CIA in the World

Since the CIA works overseas, it is important to have friendly relationships with foreign agencies. One of the closest relationships the CIA has is with Great Britain's intelligence agency **MI-6**. The two agencies often work together and share information with each other.

They work together to stop terrorist attacks in Europe and in the United States. The CIA also works closely with the International Criminal Police Organization (Interpol) as it gathers information about threats from foreign governments.

The MI-6 headquarters is located in London, England.

Another example of the CIA working well with foreign countries is Israel. Israel's intelligence agency is called the **"Mossad."** Although not as close a friendship as with MI-6, the CIA and Mossad have worked together many times.

The motto of the Mossad is "For by wise guidance you can wage your war."

In 2004, bombs exploded in the Madrid subway system. **193** people were killed and more than **2,000** wounded. The CIA helped Spanish authorities investigate.

To help people escape from East Berlin into West Berlin during the **Cold War**, tunnels were built under the Berlin Wall. One of the most famous of these tunnels is "Tunnel 57" which helped **57** people escape.

Since **1999**, the CIA has helped other agencies in the war against **ISIS** terrorists.

CIA Today

The CIA works to keep up with a changing world. New technology causes many difficulties for today's CIA. For example, today almost everyone has a smartphone or a computer. This both helps and hinders the CIA. On the one hand, people can talk to each other much more easily, even around the world. However, we also know that many terrorist use them to share information.

The wars in Iraq, Afghanistan, and Syria are changing the agency. These wars all use CIA resources. As a result, the agency needs many more agents. However, this is not all. These wars force the CIA to focus more on a military role rather than just information gathering. The CIA has had to change with the world ever since its beginning as the COI. Adapting to change and the unexpected is what the CIA does.

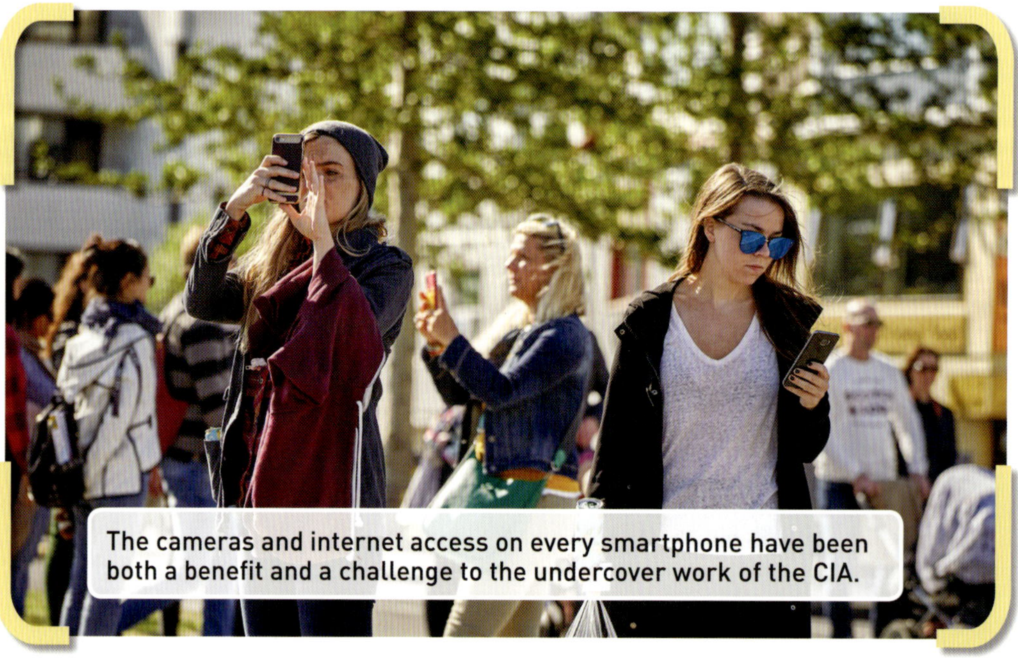

The cameras and internet access on every smartphone have been both a benefit and a challenge to the undercover work of the CIA.

Iran-Contra

MODERN CASE STUDY

From 1981–85, the CIA worked on an illegal plan. This plan involved the countries of Iran and Nicaragua. During this period, the United States did not have a very good relationship with either of these countries. The plan had two parts. The first part of the plan was to sell weapons to Iran. However, Congress had banned weapons sales to Iran. The sale was illegal.

The second part of the plan was to use that money to help fighters trying to overthrow Nicaragua's government. They were called "Contras." However, Congress had banned weapon sales to them, too. This was also illegal.

One of the key figures in the plan was marine officer Oliver North. When the plan was found out, he had to testify in front of Congress. Many other people involved did, too. Even President Reagan was in serious trouble.

By the time it was over, many government officials faced legal charges. It was known as the Iran-Contra scandal. It was the low point in President Reagan's time in office and a painful black eye for the CIA. It took a long time for the agency to regain people's trust.

Oliver North was a colonel during the Iran-Contra scandal.

The leader of Iran during the Iran-Contra scandal was Ayatollah Ruhollah Khomeni.

CIA Looking to the Future

The CIA always tries to outguess its enemies. It always tries to stay a step ahead. An important part of that is being technology experts. The CIA often has technology that the rest of the world does not know about for many years.

Planning for the future means that the CIA must deal with how fast the world is changing. While exciting, it is unpredictable. The CIA relies on predictions to keep us safe. We do not know what will happen if two different cultures suddenly meet. Would they welcome each other or go to war? How would that affect the safety in that part of the world? This type of information is the job of the CIA.

By keeping new technology for itself, the CIA can often stay ahead of any threats to the United States.

As the culture of the United States changes, the CIA needs to respond to the needs of the people.

As the world changes, there is another question. What will younger people think about old institutions like the CIA? Will they mistrust it or appreciate what it does for the United States? The CIA depends on the trust of the people to do its job. How will the agency gain their trust? The CIA is working on using technology to work on this question. The agency has entire websites designed for young people to learn about it.

One generation may have very different opinions from another. With every new generation, the CIA has to be aware of what the citizens of the United States want and need from the agency.

ACTIVITY ★★

Create a Policy Paper

The job of the CIA is to gather information from other countries that might mean to do harm to the United States. To do this, the CIA works closely with friendly nations and uses secret means to learn about hostile nations. The agency tries to influence those hostile nations to control its citizens who might attack us. We have learned that sometimes the agency has broken serious laws in its attempts to influence foreign governments.

Develop your own thoughts on how much the CIA should be able to influence a foreign government in order to protect the United States. Write a policy paper that summarizes your opinion

Step 1:

Answer the following questions to help you develop your opinion.

1. Should the CIA have to obey the laws of a foreign country? If not, why not?
2. Do you think foreigners should have to obey U.S. law? If not, why not? If so, when?
3. If a foreign government does not control its anti-U.S. citizens, what right does the United States have to force them? Does it have any?
4. Does the United States have the right to force its citizens to not speak their beliefs if they are against a foreign country?
5. Are there any methods the CIA should not use to gain information from foreigners? If so, what are they?
6. Are there any methods foreign agents should not use against U.S. citizens to gain information? If so, what are they?
7. Does the United States, as foreigners, have the right to change another nation's leaders?

Step 2:

Take your opinions from Question 1 - 7 and write a one-page policy paper. It should explain the policy you think is correct about how much the CIA should be allowed to influence a foreign government in order to protect the United States. It should also explain why. Include an introductory paragraph.

- Paragraph 1: What is the question?
- Paragraph 2: What are the issues surrounding the question?
- Paragraph 3: What is your policy on the issue, and why?

QUIZ ★★

1 The CIA must obey the rules and laws of which document?

2 What was today's CIA known as during World War II?

3 Which president created today's CIA?

4 What U.S. marine officer supported the Iran-Contra plan?

5 The right to privacy is guaranteed by which amendment to the Constitution?

6 Which U.S. agency helped the CIA investigate Pan Am flight 103?

7 Which president shut down the OSS?

8 What is the British foreign intelligence service called?

9 What is the main job of the CIA?

10 Who is the first female director of the CIA?

ANSWERS

1. Constitution 2. OSS 3. Harry Truman 4. Oliver North 5. Fourth Amendment 6. FBI 7. Harry Truman 8. MI-6 9. To gather information on foreign countries 10. Gina Haspel

KEY WORDS ★★

Cold War: hostility that existed between the Soviet Union and the United States from 1945 to 1991

counterintelligence: a program of a government or other organization to frustrate enemy espionage

classified: secret. Only certain authorized people have access to this information.

diplomat: an official that represents a country

double-agents: a spy who pretends to act for one country while in fact acting on behalf of an enemy

legislative: a group of people with the authority to make laws for a political entity, such as a country or city

MI-6: the foreign intelligence service of the government of Great Britain

Mossad: the national intelligence agency of Israel

popular sovereignty: the principle that the authority of a state and its government are controlled by the people of the state

reconnaissance: gathering information

Soviet Union: a socialist state in Eurasia that existed from 1922 to 1991

spies: people who secretly collect and report information on the activities, movements, and plans of an enemy or competitor

terrorist: a person who uses violence and intimidation, especially against civilians, for political reasons

INDEX ★★

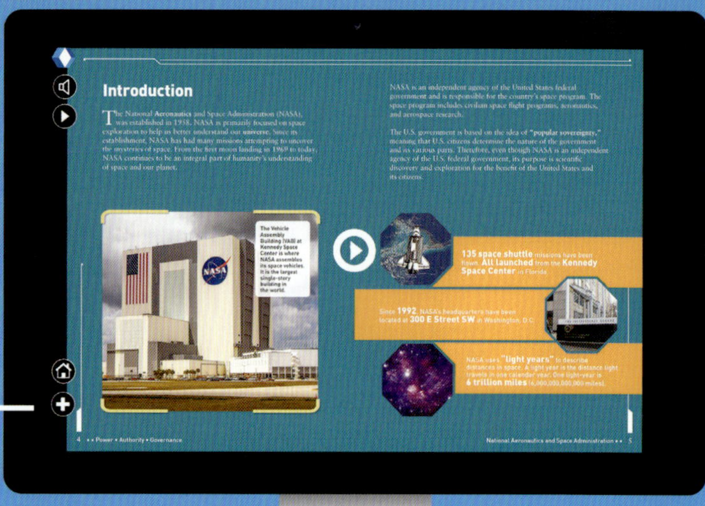

SUPPLEMENTARY RESOURCES

Click on the plus icon ⊕ found in the bottom left corner of each spread to open additional teacher resources.

- Download and print the book's quizzes and activities
- Access curriculum correlations
- Explore additional web applications that enhance the Lightbox experience

LIGHTBOX DIGITAL TITLES
Packed full of integrated media

VIDEOS

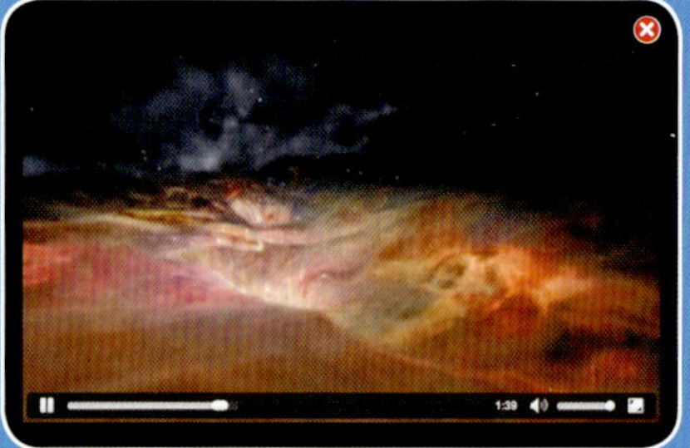

INTERACTIVE MAPS

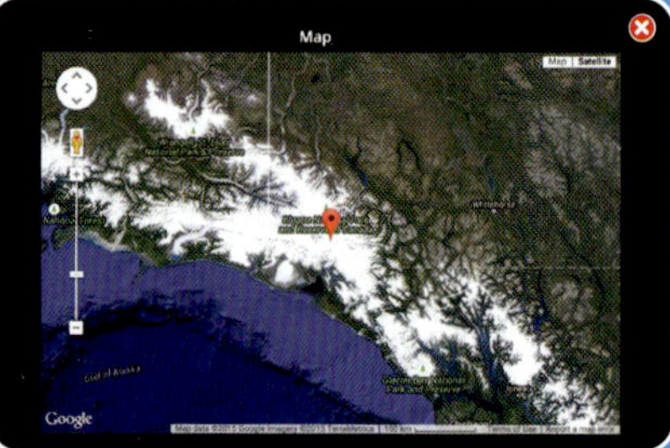

WEBLINKS

SLIDESHOWS

QUIZZES

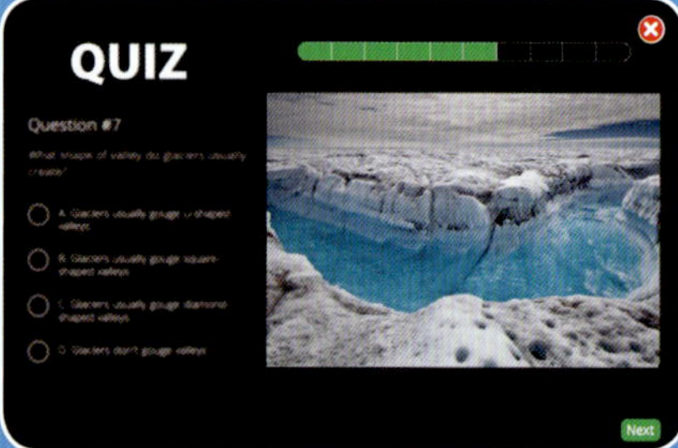

OPTIMIZED FOR

- ✔ TABLETS
- ✔ WHITEBOARDS
- ✔ COMPUTERS
- ✔ AND MUCH MORE!

Published by Smartbook Media Inc.
350 5th Avenue, 59th Floor New York, NY 10118
Website: www.openlightbox.com

Copyright © 2020 Smartbook Media Inc.
All rights reserved. No part of this publication may be reproduced, stored in a retrieval system, or transmitted in any form or by any means, electronic, mechanical, photocopying, recording, or otherwise, without the prior written permission of the publisher.

Library of Congress Control Number: 2019939793

ISBN 978-1-5105-4680-6 (hardcover)
ISBN 978-1-5105-4682-0 (multi-user eBook)

Printed in Guangzhou, China
1 2 3 4 5 6 7 8 9 0 23 22 21 20 19

052019
122718

Editor: John Willis
Art Director: Terry Paulhus

Every reasonable effort has been made to trace ownership and to obtain permission to reprint copyright material. The publisher would be pleased to have any errors or omissions brought to its attention so that they may be corrected in subsequent printings.

The publisher acknowledges Alamy, Shutterstock, and Wikimedia Commons as its primary image suppliers for this title.